OLDSMOBILE

1946-1960 PHOTO ARCHIVE

Byron Olsen

Iconografix

PHOTO ARCHIVE SERIES

Iconografix
PO Box 446
Hudson, Wisconsin 54016 USA

Library of Congress Control Number: 2006921108

ISBN-13: 978-1-58388-168-2
ISBN-10: 1-58388-168-9

06 07 08 09 10 11 6 5 4 3 2 1

Printed in China

Cover and book design by Dan Perry

Cover photo- A happy couple setting out for a Sunday drive in their new 1949 Olds 98 convertible. In 1949, it just didn't get much better than this.

BOOK PROPOSALS

Iconografix is a publishing company specializing in books for transportation enthusiasts. We publish in a number of different areas, including Automobiles, Auto Racing, Buses, Construction Equipment, Emergency Equipment, Farming Equipment, Railroads & Trucks. The Iconografix imprint is constantly growing and expanding into new subject areas.

Authors, editors, and knowledgeable enthusiasts in the field of transportation history are invited to contact the Editorial Department at Iconografix, Inc., PO Box 446, Hudson, WI 54016.

Acknowledgments

Most of the photographs in this book originally came from the company files of Oldsmobile Division of General Motors. Some came from the files of competitive auto manufacturers. All photos used are now the property of the National Automotive History Collection (NAHC) of the Detroit Public Library, Detroit, Michigan. The author would like to express his special thanks to the NAHC and Mark Patrick, Curator, for sharing these pieces of automobile history and helping to make this book possible.

Bibliography

Oldsmobile: The Postwar Years, Jan P. Norbye and Jim Dunne, Motorbooks International (1981)
The Cars of Oldsmobile, Dennis Casteele, Crestline Publishing (1981)
Standard Catalog of American Cars (4th Edition), Edited by Ron Kowalke, Krause Publications (1997)
Oldsmobile Sales Literature from all years 1946 through 1960, Author's Collection
A Century of Automotive Style, Michael Lamm and Dave Holls, Lamm-Morada Publishing Co. (1996)
The Production Figure Book for U.S. Cars, Jerry Heasley, Motorbooks International (1977)
Oldsmobile Buyer's Guide, Richard Langworth, Motorbooks International (1987)

Introduction

This is not a book about the history of Oldsmobile Division of General Motors. Several others have already done that. This is a book for the Oldsmobile enthusiast who wants a closer look at the Oldsmobiles built in the years covered by this book. It is for people restoring an Olds built in one of those years. It is also for people interested in auto history who want a more detailed look at Oldsmobile products than is usually afforded by a book concentrating on a text about company history.

Thus, it is assumed that a reader of this book already has access to Olds corporate history. Nevertheless, the captions in this book mention some historic highlights to provide a context for the photos. These photos show Oldsmobiles in detail and views of models seldom seen. Most are from 8 x 10 originals, which gives a level of clarity not often seen today. They are truly a photo archive and a more accurate visual historic reference than photos of restored cars. All of the photos in this book were originally taken by, or for, Oldsmobile Division, or by competing automobile companies. They were all taken when the cars shown were brand new. Many photos show the cars the way the manufacturer thought they should be seen.

Oldsmobile was started by one of the foremost pioneers of the auto industry, Ransom Eli Olds. Olds built engines for boats and stationary power uses for several years before he built his first car. His early success was the curved dash runabout, a simple, low priced car that many could afford. Olds also pioneered some of the first efforts to develop the production line. Olds was an early champion of the concept that automobiles should be widely popularized by keeping them simple and lowering the cost as much as possible. In this, he was several years ahead of Henry Ford, who developed that concept to huge success with the Model T Ford. After the curved dash was a success, Olds had a falling out with his financial backers, and left Olds Motor Works in 1905. He was never again associated with the car that bore his name, although he immediately founded REO (the name uses his initials) and went on building automobiles until 1937. After Olds left the Company, Oldsmobile was acquired by General Motors, where it soon became established as a mainstay of GM's medium priced offerings.

This book covers some interesting years for Oldsmobile, from 1946 through 1960. In the thirties and forties, Olds was considered the experimental division of General Motors. Oldsmobile pioneered the Automatic Safety Transmission in 1937. It was the precursor to Hydra-Matic Drive, the first fully automatic transmission, which Olds introduced to the world in 1940. There would not be another fully automatic transmission until 1948, when Buick's Dynaflow was introduced.

By the end of World War II in 1945, Oldsmobile had a solid, but not very exciting reputation in the industry. All that soon changed, as the postwar era unfolded, and as this book chronicles. Exciting new postwar body designs, and the breathtaking new Rocket engine in 1949, transformed the Oldsmobile image. These developments also transformed Oldsmobile sales, doubling them by 1950 and tripling them by 1955.

This book also shows the unfortunate designs of 1957 and 1958 and the beginnings of the road to recovery as exemplified by the 1959 and 1960 models. Olds in the sixties and seventies would go from success to success (with some bumps along the way) culminating in several years in the seventies when Olds built over one million cars a year (1977-1979). All of this glorious history made terminating the marque seem almost inexplicable when the end came in 2004, over 100 years after the marque was born.

I must confess to some bias. I have owned one of Oldsmobile's finest models for 25 years, a 1949 Rocket engined 98 convertible, the same model shown on the cover of this book. It still looks and performs beautifully, and proudly. It is a magnificent car and to me will always exemplify the creative spirit of the people who made Oldsmobile a great car.

Byron Olsen
December 23, 2005

After World War II ended in 1945, car builders put 1942 models back in production with minimal changes. There wasn't time to engineer any major modifications, and a car-starved public didn't care; no cars had been built for four years and the old ones were wearing out. But Olds presented a striking new grill—simpler, cleaner and looking very futuristic. It would set the pattern for a decade of Oldsmobile grills. This is a 1946 Series 70 which Olds called the "Dynamic Cruiser."

This is a 1946 Series 70 two-door which Olds called a Club Sedan. It rode a hefty 125-inch wheelbase and was available with either an L head six- or an in-line L head eight-cylinder engine. The wrap-around bumpers were a postwar development. There were two body styles available in the Series 70, both fastbacks—the Club Sedan and the four-door sedan, as shown on this page.

Oldsmobile in the forties built cars using all three sizes of bodies produced by General Motors. This is a Series 60 fastback Club Sedan. The body and rear deck are shorter than the Series 70 shown on the previous page. Series 60 Oldsmobiles used a 119-inch wheelbase and shared the General Motors "A" bodies with Chevrolet and Pontiac.

A 1946 Olds Series 60 four-door. The Series 60 was available only with the 100-horsepower 238-cubic-inch six-cylinder in 1946. The 110-horsepower 257-cid straight eight became available in this series starting in 1947. In addition to the models shown here, a club coupe was also available in the 60 Series. In this first year of postwar production with strikes and material shortages, Olds built 119,388 cars.

A 1946 Series 60 station wagon. Like most wagons of the forties, body and roof were entirely built of wood with a fabric roof covering. These bodies were built for Olds by Ionia and Hercules, both independent station wagon body builders who built for other car manufacturers as well. Body styling varied considerably between the two suppliers. Second and third seats had to be unbolted and lifted out to make room for more cargo.

This sporty 1946 convertible was available in the 60 Series. Power top operation was standard and this was only the second year that Olds convertibles were built with rear quarter windows. Hydra-Matic fully automatic transmission, pioneered by Oldsmobile in 1940, was an option on all models. The white wheel trim discs were an early postwar substitute for white sidewall tires, which were not immediately available after the war.

The sleek rear end of a 1946 Series 70 four-door sedan, with an attractive two-tone paint scheme. The small rear window was one drawback of the fast back body style. The Series 70 used the GM "B" body, shared with some Pontiacs, smaller Buicks, and the Cadillac Series 61. The trunk emblems tell us that this car is equipped with an eight-cylinder engine and Hydra-Matic drive. This style of taillight was used on most Series 60 and 70 models in 1946 and 1947.

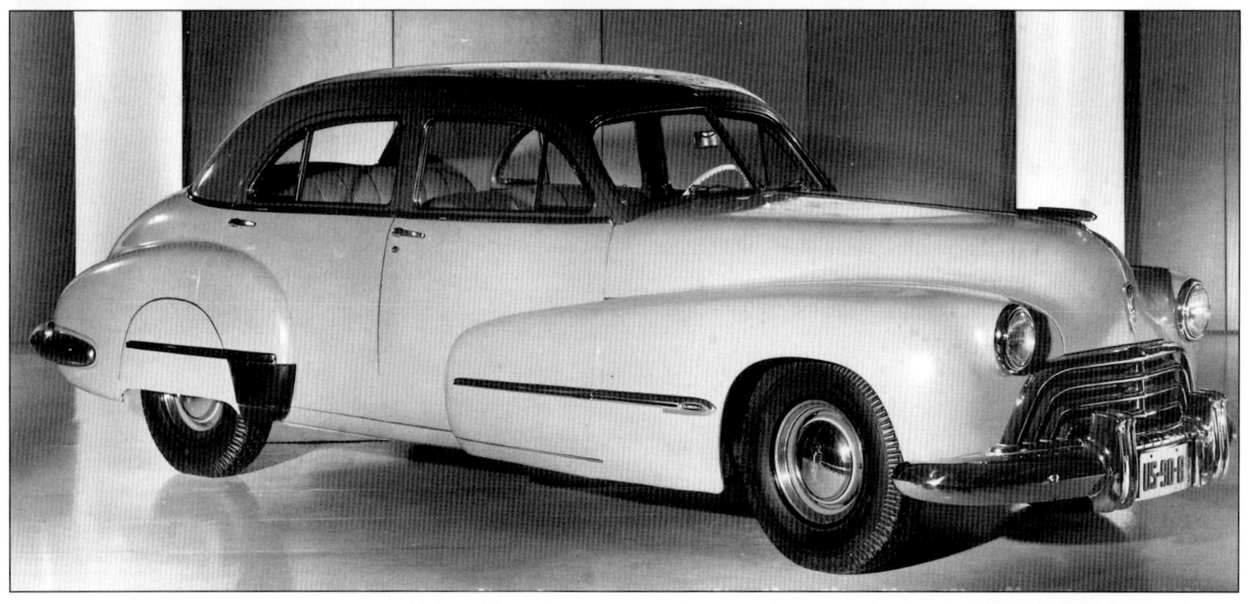

The top of the Oldsmobile line-up for 1946, a Series 98 Custom 8 Cruiser sedan. The 98s used the large GM "C" body shared with the larger Cadillac and Buick models. The 98 wheelbase was also longer, at 127 inches. The 110-horsepower Olds straight eight was standard on the 98. Also available were a 98 convertible and fastback club sedan.

The bold new grill of the postwar Oldsmobiles, here seen on a 1947 model. The parking and turn lights housed in the bumper guards were another feature unique to the 1946-1948 Oldsmobiles. This grill set the pattern for a decade of Oldsmobile grill designs.

About the only exterior change for 1947 was a slight redesign of the front fender rub rail. This is a Series 60 Club sedan otherwise unchanged from 1946, except that the eight-cylinder engine could now be ordered. A club coupe was also available.

A 1947 Series 60 four-door sedan. Wheelbase remained 119 inches. When the six-cylinder was specified, it was called a "66," and when the eight was ordered, it was a "68."

Series 70 cars, such as this 1947 Club Sedan, were also referred to as "76" or "78," depending on which engine was ordered. Judging by the white painted trim rings on these 1947 models, white sidewall tires were still hard to come by. 1947 Oldsmobile output improved to 194,388 cars.

This is the glamour leader of the 1947 Oldsmobile line, a Series 98 convertible. After the war, six-cylinder engines were no longer available in the Series 90, so there were no more models referred to as "96s." These convertibles had hydraulic powered tops, front seats and door windows as standard equipment.

The 1948 models were given a few more styling tweaks to differentiate them from previous models. Interiors and paint colors were revised, taillights were changed, and the front fender rub rail was again changed. But it took a sharp eye to distinguish a 48 from a 47. This is a Series 60 four-door. At least whitewall tires were finally back.

This 1948 Series 60 station wagon carries a completely different body than the 1946 and 1947 Olds wagons. This one has one, instead of two, decorative horizontal side wood trim strips and a smaller and less complex belt line wood molding. Some sources claim that Ionia and Hercules both supplied Olds bodies during this period, but another source states that Fisher is the builder of this one. The outside sun visor is a dealer-installed accessory. Visors were popular for a few years during the late forties and early fifties as windshield design began to increase the slant of the glass.

Another look at the revised 1948 Olds wagon. The roof line curved up more than its predecessors, and the tailgate now had a curve to it, but was more nearly vertical. Compare this to the wagon shown on Page 8. These bodies were still constructed entirely of wood including the roof, which was fabric covered. It was still common for wagons to have but one taillight.

The Series 70 benefited from new interiors and colors as well, but was unchanged mechanically. This is a 1948 Series 70 four-door.

This is a view of a Series 70 four-door rear fender showing the new vertical taillights for 1948. These lights were also used on the Series 60 cars, except wagons. This car was equipped with optional fender skirts.

The big news at Olds for 1948 was a completely new Series 98. This was the first new postwar body design from GM and was shared only with Cadillac. Glass area was greatly increased, the windshield was now curved and the front fender line flowed all the way to the rear of the car. The wheelbase was slightly shorter at 125 inches and power still came from the venerable 110-horsepower straight eight. But more power was on the way for 1949.

This rear view of the 98 sedan shows the large two-piece curved glass rear window and the low slung taper of the deck and rear fenders. Unlike some postwar car designs that were beginning to appear, the rear fender contour was still prominently displayed. Oldsmobile coined the word "Futuramic" to describe the new models.

A handsome 1948 Series 98 convertible. Although not a hot performer with the old straight eight, the new models sold well. Production of the 98 Series almost doubled, going from 37,148 in 1947 to 65,235 in 1948. Clearly the motoring public welcomed some fresh new automotive styling. Total Olds output for 1948 was 173,661 cars of all three series.

1949 would turn out to be a banner year for Oldsmobile Division. With new bodies for the smaller models, and a hot new engine, the reputation of Olds as a stodgy performer with conservative styling was changed overnight. Shown is the brand new Series 76 club coupe with its L head six enlarged to 257 cid. Horsepower was upped to 105 bhp.

Here is the star performer and the really big news for Olds in 1949: the Rocket V8 engine. This was the very first of a new generation of short stroke, high compression, overhead valve V8 engines that forever changed Detroit engine design. Within six years, every U.S. car builder would follow the lead of Oldsmobile and offer an OHV V8. The Rocket, at 303 cid, was 25 percent larger than its predecessor and a whole lot more powerful at 135 bhp. The new engine helped boost model year output to 288,310 cars, a new record for Olds.

The Rocket V8 was originally intended only for the Series 98. The Series 76 was intended to be the only smaller Oldsmobile. A last minute decision to offer the Rocket in the 76 chassis created a legend and changed Oldsmobile forever. Christened the "88," here is the same coupe model shown on Page 19, packing 135 eager V8 horses under the hood. In 1949, the only identification for the 88 was in the forward rocker panel molding which said "Futuramic," as shown here, and sometimes carried the 88 numerals above.

The most popular 88 was the four-door sedan, and as it blazed away from stoplights at the head of the pack all over North America, everyone knew a new legend had been born. The new 88 would do zero to 60 in about 12 seconds, and was the hottest 1949 American car.

Every model in the Series 76 range was available as an 88. This is an 88 Club Sedan available also as a four-door in fastback form. The Olds 76 and 88 used the General Motors "A" body shell, also shared with Chevrolet and Pontiac. Available body types included four-door sedans, (both notchback and fast back), fastback two-door club sedans, club coupes, convertibles, and station wagons. These two series replaced the Series 60 and 70 of prior years and used a 119-inch wheelbase. The new 88 roughly tripled sales of eight-cylinder engines in these two series over 1948.

This shows the handsome rear view of the 76 and 88, in this case a notchback four-door sedan. The emblem on the deck lid shows that this car is equipped with Hydra-Matic, which was standard on all Rocket engine cars in 1949.

The tailgate view of an early 49 Olds real wood wagon. Note the rods below the taillights, which pivoted the taillights when the tailgate was open so that they continued to show light to the rear.

A 1949 Series 76 station wagon. 1949 was a transitional year in wagon design, as car builders began moving from wood to steel construction. This Olds is a good example. The roof was now steel, and the full-fendered design reduced room for wood work on the sides. Olds (and most other GM wagons) switched from the partial wood construction shown here to all steel construction in mid-year.

The Pace Car Olds 88 convertible even had a unique leather interior. The bench type rear seat armrests were typical of GM convertibles of the time, but everything else was special for this car.

A shining moment for Oldsmobile in 1949, when the hot new 88 was selected as Pace Car for the Indianapolis 500 mile race. A specially trimmed 88 convertible was set up for the occasion with a unique rocket ornament on the front fenders.

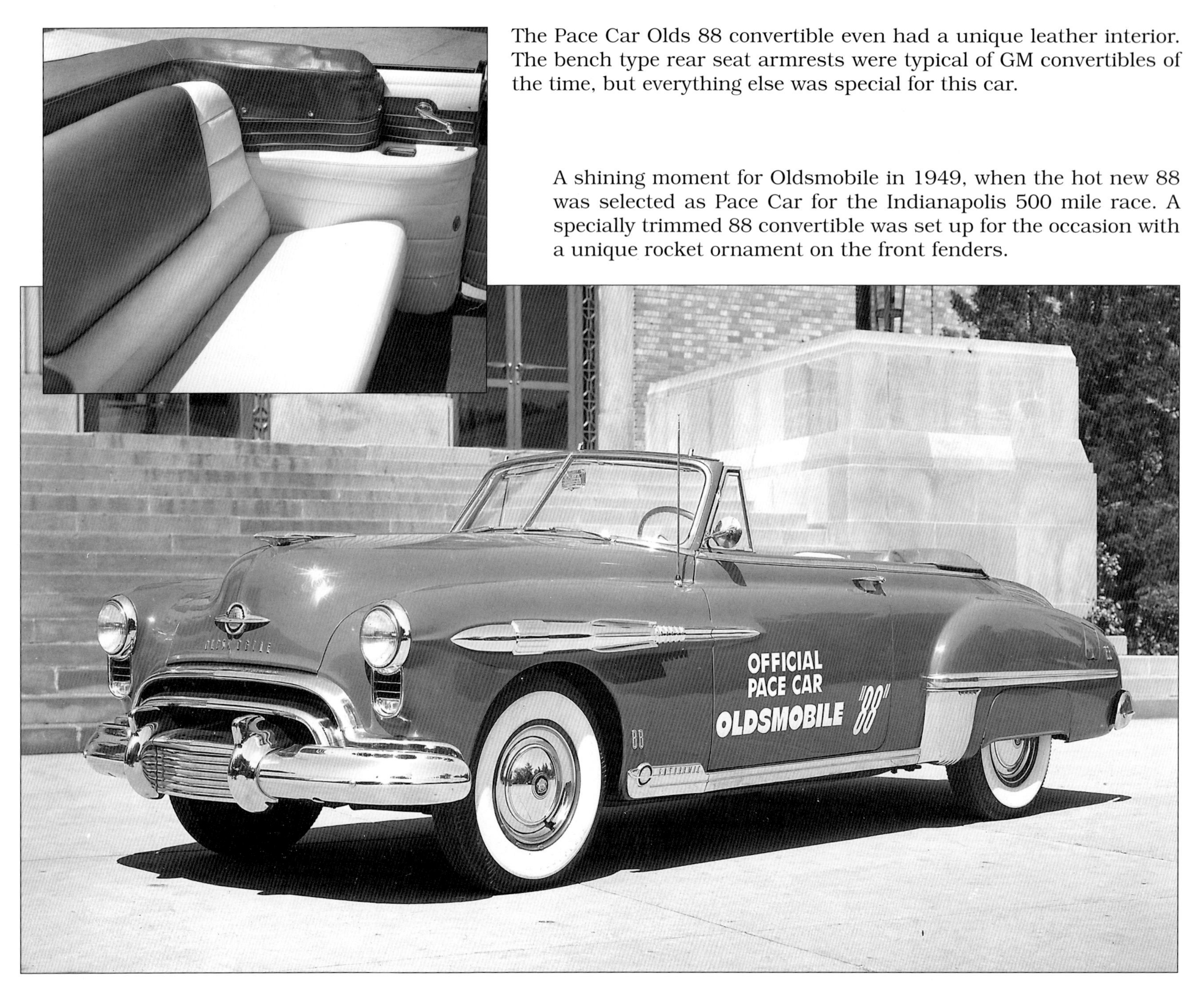

The 98 had received a brand new body in 1948. Now, for 1949, it got the hot new Rocket engine under the hood. In an unusual move for the times, stylists even removed some chrome trim for 1949. The rub rail on the front fender was replaced with a rocker panel plaque which said "Futuramic."

The rear view of the 1949 98 shows only minor changes from the 1948 models. The sedan rear window was made one piece, and there were discreet chrome fins placed on top of the rear fenders. A squared-off trunk lid permitted the spare tire to be stored upright and increased luggage space.

This is the plush interior of a 1949 Oldsmobile 98 sedan with the De Luxe equipment option. Fabric was dark gray broadcloth with striped fabric inserts. The folding center armrest was only provided with the De Luxe equipment option, which was chosen by the vast majority of 98 buyers. Passengers in an Olds 98 were riding in the same body as travelers in a Cadillac.

This is the modern dash and interior of a 1949 98. Note that instruments and controls are grouped in front of the driver instead of being spread across the dashboard. Shown is a convertible interior. 98s were available as a four-door, a two-door fastback (club sedan), a convertible, and later in the model year, a two-door hardtop. 98 sales rose 50 percent over 1948.

An elegant and stylish 1949 Oldsmobile 98 convertible coupe. Upholstery was all leather or a combination of leather and Bedford cord in a variety of color choices. All windows, the top and the front seat were hydraulically operated. Powerplant was of course the 135 horsepower Rocket V8 with Hydra-Matic transmission.

A sleek 1949 98 Club Sedan, looking almost sinister with its sweeping lines and black wall tires. The reverse angled rear pillar gave rear seat occupants some extra visibility while preserving the privacy unique to this body type. But fastbacks were fading in popularity and would be gone from the Olds line in just two more years.

In mid-1949, GM introduced a new body style which became known as the "hardtop convertible." These new hardtops had fixed steel roofs which did not fold down, but used convertible style windows. When rolled down, there was no body post left standing behind the door. These models also introduced wrap-around rear windows to enhance the open car feel. Hardtops were announced almost simultaneously by Buick, Cadillac and Oldsmobile. All three used the same body. The Oldsmobile version, shown here, was called the "Holiday" and was part of the 98 series. The new body type was an instant hit and soon swept the industry.

For 1950, the Series 76 and 88 models were little changed. The 76 Series was continued, but its days were numbered. With the huge success of the 88, Sherrod Skinner, General Manager of Oldsmobile Division, discontinued the 76 in mid-year after only 33,257 had been produced. The 76 was supposed to be the Olds economy model, but most buyers wanted the Rocket under the hood. This is a 76 Club Coupe.

A 76 four-door sedan. For 1950, the fastback four-door was discontinued, and a notchback two-door and Holiday hard-top added to both the 76 and 88 lines. The 76 could now be easily distinguished from the 88 by lack of front fender trim and different taillights. Other body styles available in both 76 and 88 (they shared the same bodies) were a convertible, wagon, and fastback two-door.

The station wagon for 1950 continued the all steel construction started with the late 1949 wagons. The contours stamped in the steel panels were finished with imitation wood graining so that it was difficult to distinguish them from the early 1949 partly wood predecessors. This is a Series 76. Skinner discontinued the wagon body style in mid-year, just as the wagon body type was beginning to catch on with families.

The big news at Olds continued to be the 88 Series with its hot Rocket engine. The style leader for all Olds series was the new Holiday hardtop model seen here in 88 form. The 88 models now carried a bright metal trim strip that extended from the headlight rim over most of the front door. Production of 1950 88s soared to a stunning 268,412 cars.

This 1950 88 four-door shows off another piece of new trim for this Series. A chromium crown was added to the back fender just above and forward of the taillights. This piece carried the numbers "88" on the side and served to provide instant identification. They also housed back up lights, if ordered.

A 1950 88 two-door fastback club sedan tricked out to show off the Rocket engine. The oversize Rocket hood ornament and sign on the door called attention to the new engine, which could be viewed through the transparent hood panel. This is an early production 88 with a two-piece windshield. The switch to a one-piece windshield on 88s was made during the 1950 production run.

This notchback two-door sedan was a new addition to the 88 and 76 lines for 1950. It proved popular, and led to the disappearance of the fastback club sedan after 1950. This one is an 88.

The real glamour leader of 1950 and any other year is usually the convertible, and this 1950 88 was no exception. Sporting large 7.60 x 15 white sidewall tires, the people and the car look ready for some cruising.

The Olds 98 got a completely new body for 1950. The new GM "C" body, which the 98 shared with Buick and Cadillac, had lower, wider front fenders which gave it a massive, heavy look. Wheelbase was reduced from 125 to 122 inches. This is a Holiday hardtop.

The 1950 Olds 98 was available in two fastback body styles: a two-door club sedan, seen here, and a four-door version. Both sold poorly. The fastback style, very popular in the forties, disappeared completely from the Oldsmobile line after 1950.

The hands down sales leader of the 98 Series was the notchback four-door sedan seen here. The lower and wider fenders show up in this photo. This model accounted for over 80,000 of the 106,220 98s built for 1950. Olds built a stunning total of 407,889 1950 model cars.

The 98 sedan seen from the rear. The back window was now three-piece and wrapped around to the body sides. The rear door window area was squared off in an unusually abrupt fashion. Hydra-Matic was standard equipment on most 1950 Oldsmobiles, although a manual transmission could be ordered.

The big news for Olds in 1951 was a new model, the Super 88. Shown here in Holiday (hardtop) form, the new car used the new General Motors "B" body, which it shared with Buick Special. The Super 88 immediately became the flagship of the line.

The new Super 88 body was slightly larger, with a one-piece windshield, and a dashboard that continued the previous design theme. The chromium ribs covering the radio speaker in the center and the glove box were now vertical instead of horizontal.

This is a 1951 Super 88 two-door. The use of the name "club sedan" was dropped, as were all fastback models. A club coupe was still available, in addition to the other models shown here. Although only slightly larger than the model it replaced, the new body appeared heftier and taller.

The Super 88 four-door sedan. The outside sun visor as shown on this car was an accessory already fading in popularity. Hydra-Matic Drive was an option, but found its way into almost every Oldsmobile.

A rear view of the Super 88 four-door sedan, showing the rather ornate rocket inspired taillights and large trunk. This was the best selling 88 body type, accounting for more than one-third of all Super 88 sales.

This is the sportiest Super 88, the convertible. Horsepower of the Rocket engine remained at 135 bhp, although the horsepower race of the fifties would soon come to Oldsmobile.

The original 88 body design was continued through the 1951 model year as the lower cost standard model Series 88. It took the place of the Series 76, which had been dropped the previous year. Interior trim was plain and a few amenities were omitted (note that the rear quarter vent wings no longer open), but on the outside it appeared unchanged.

The only other body style available in the standard 88 was the two-door sedan, shown here. This lower cost Series used the same engine as the more expensive Oldsmobiles, the 135 bhp Rocket V8. This Series was discontinued before the end of the model year.

The 98 body, new in 1950, is shown here in 1951 trim. The wide, low fenders and high hood are particularly evident here. The grills under the headlights were functional and served as fresh air intakes for heating and ventilation.

A good deal of bright metal trim was added to the 98 for 1951. The side rub rail became full length and a large spear was added to the rear fender.

The rear view of the 98 sedan, which became the best selling model in the entire Oldsmobile line at over 78,000 cars. The abrupt angle at the back of the rear door window was masked in 1951 by a new chrome panel.

Here is a handsome 1951 98 Holiday hardtop. The unique coil spring Oldsmobile rear suspension was replaced in 1951 with a more conventional (and cheaper) leaf spring Hotchkiss drive layout in the Super 88 and 98 models. The lower priced standard 88 continued to use the coil spring suspension, which actually caused the rear end to rise up on acceleration instead of squatting, and controlled front end "dive" on braking.

Another 1951 Olds 98 at its most glamorous in convertible form. Hydraulic power windows were standard on the 98 Holidays and convertibles and optional on the Super 88. Total Olds production for the 1951 model year came to 285,615 cars, down somewhat from 1950 due in part to the start of the Korean war.

For 1952, the big news was a redesigned Series 98, which now used the same body as the Super 88. The woman in the photo is pointing to the principal difference, a rear deck nine inches longer. The 98 wheelbase was also stretched four inches over the Super 88 to 124 inches. This is a Holiday hardtop.

Here is a 98 four-door sedan showing off the new long trunk. Power steering became available as an option on all Oldsmobiles. Olds began spelling out the name of its top line series instead of using numerals. The "Ninety-eight" was also referred to as "Classic."

This is the rear seat of a 1952 Ninety-eight sedan. The upholstery was very luxurious with a folding center armrest, and was available in gray or green broadcloth. The wrap-around rear window was now one piece.

The longer deck on the Ninety-eights was particularly evident on the convertible, shown here. The Hydra-Matic transmission now provided an additional gear selection range permitting the car to be held in third gear for city and mountain driving. This new range was called “Super” drive and was marked “S” on the transmission selector quadrant.

The 1952 Super 88s were little changed from the previous year. In addition to the Holiday shown here, Super 88s were available as a convertible, four-door and two-door sedans, and a club coupe. It would be the last year for the club coupe body style as the Holiday hardtop was stealing most of the coupe's sales.

Here is a Super 88 four-door sedan. This was Oldsmobile's best selling model, with over 70,000 built. Total Oldsmobile production for the 1952 model year reached 213,419 cars, down again, but good for fourth place in the industry.

The Super 88 could be distinguished from the lower priced De Luxe 88 by the bright chrome sash on the rear fender. This is a Super 88 two-door sedan. Horsepower in the Super 88s and Ninety-eights was upped to 160 bhp primarily through use of a four-barrel carburetor. Displacement remained at 303 cid.

The 1952 De Luxe 88 used the same body as the Super 88 with less brightwork and smaller taillights. It also used a less powerful engine developing 145 horsepower due to use of a two-barrel carburetor. All Oldsmobiles now used the same body.

The De Luxe 88, seen here in two-door form, omitted fender skirts, which were standard on the Super 88s. This Series was available only as a two-door or four-door sedan and were the lowest price Oldsmobiles.

For 1953, Oldsmobile continued to use the body shell introduced on the 1951 Super 88 on all models. Exterior trim was cleaned up, hoods and decks were squared off, and the dashboard was redesigned. The bumper guards now appeared to be air intakes, but were not.

This is a 1953 De Luxe 88 two-door, Oldsmobile's lowest priced car. Prices for this model started at just $2,065 at the factory. Horsepower had inched up to 150 bhp. Engine displacement was still 303 cid, and this Series still used a two-barrel carburetor.

This side view of a Super 88 shows the squared off hood and deck on the 1953 models, and also shows the additional trim on this more expensive model. Two amenities on this series were opening rear quarter vent windows, and fender skirts.

A very sharp looking 1953 Super 88 convertible. Super 88 horsepower had been raised slightly to 165 bhp. This Series, and the 98s used a four barrel carburetor. All Oldsmobiles switched to 12-volt electrical systems, along with Cadillac and Buick. The rest of the industry followed by 1956.

The Super 88 line was reduced to just four body types: the Holiday hardtop shown here, a convertible, and two- and four-door sedans. Other big news in the option department was the arrival of power brakes and air conditioning.

This happy driver is enjoying air conditioning in her new Ninety-eight sedan. The evaporator was mounted in the trunk and air distributed through ceiling mounted ducts and outlets, one of which can be seen here.

The new instrument panel featured a round gauge cluster and a center-mounted glove compartment. The car shown is equipped with the new power brake option: note the low pedal. Another option seen here on the top left side of the dash is the Autronic Eye, an automatic headlight dimmer first introduced in 1952.

Here is a 1953 Ninety-eight four-door sedan, demonstrating its newly squared off hood profile and more restrained rear fender trim. All in all, this is a handsome car.

An equally handsome Ninety-eight Holiday. There were two other Ninety-eight models, both convertibles. Total Oldsmobile production for the 1953 model year reached 334,462, up substantially from the previous year.

Mid-year, the glamorous Fiesta convertible was introduced. It was a modified Ninety-eight convertible showcasing the first use in a production car of a wrap-around windshield (along with the Cadillac Eldorado). The price was almost double the cost of the Ninety-eight convertible ($5,715 compared to $2,983). As one might expect with this price difference, only 458 were built, compared to over 7,500 Ninety-eight convertibles.

This is the luxurious interior of the Fiesta. Several leather trim combinations unique to the Fiesta were available to harmonize with the special exterior colors. The engine was rated at 5 more horsepower than other Oldsmobiles.

Another view of the striking Fiesta, at an auto show surrounded by other 1953 model cars. That is a Studebaker on the right and a Pontiac in the distance. The cut down doors and special trim of the Fiesta are evident here.

This is the Olds Starfire, a one-off concept car that was shown at auto shows during the 1953 model year. Made of fiber-glass and fully operational, the Starfire foretold significant design features of the 1954 and later models, including the wrap-around windshield and the rear fender shape.

The radically redesigned 1954 Oldsmobiles were a stunning departure from previous models. The most obvious change was the wrap-around windshield, which Olds referred to as "panoramic." Yet the grill design continued earlier themes and was quickly recognizable. This is a Super 88 Holiday coupe.

Another major departure was the raised fender line and lower, flatter hood profile. This is a Super 88 two-door. The height of most body styles was at least three inches lower and glass area was increased by almost 300 square inches over previous models. This striking new GM body shell was shared with Buick Special and Century.

A profile view of the best selling 1954 Olds, the Super 88 four-door sedan. This model sold over 111,000 cars. The radical curvature of the new windshield and the changed contour of the windshield post are evident here. Power was raised to 185 horsepower, thanks to an engine displacement increase from 303 cid to 324 cid.

Yet another striking styling change was the dropped side window sill line, especially noticeable on hard-tops and convertibles. This Super 88 convertible looks especially sporty. Wheelbase of all 88 models was increased to 122 inches. Oldsmobile claimed that the 1954 cars were originally intended to be the 1955 models.

This photo graphically demonstrates the interference created by the new shape of the windshield post. It doesn't seem to bother this young woman, but would eventually doom the wrap-around windshield. This is a Super 88 hardtop, identified by the "88" emblem above the rear fender trim.

The lowest priced 1954 Oldsmobile was now called simply the "88" and was virtually indistinguishable from the Super 88. The interior was less luxurious, but on the outside only the location of the "88" numerals below the rear fender trim strip revealed its identity. Horsepower of this Series was slightly less at 170 bhp. This Holiday coupe model was a new addition to this line.

Although the Ninety-eight continued to use the same body as the 88, wheel base was 126 inches, four inches longer, and overall length was a commanding 214 inches, 9 inches longer than the 88. All of this extra length went into the rear deck. The scoops over the taillights were air intakes for the optional air-conditioning system.

The Ninety-eight Holiday and convertible had unique side trim and more fully cut out wheel openings with no fender skirts. The chrome strip down the center of the trunk lid was inspired by the 1953 Fiesta. This is a 98 Holiday hardtop.

The 1954 Ninety-eight convertible was named “Starfire” after the concept car from the year before. But with its cut down doors and panoramic windshield, it was really the equivalent of the previous year’s Fiesta convertible.

The big news at Olds for 1955 was the arrival of a new body type, the four-door hardtop. Available in both 88 and Ninety-eight lines, the glamorous new style helped Oldsmobile set a new all time production record of 583,179 cars. This is the Super 88 version.

This is the Ninety-eight Holiday hardtop sedan. Like the Ninety-eight two-door hardtops and convertibles, the four-door version also used scooped out wheel openings and no fender skirts. The Holiday four-door hardtop sedans were introduced January 6, 1955, two months after the rest of the line.

To clear the overlapping front door window and the door hinge mechanisms, the rear door window had to back up, as shown here, before lowering.

The four-door hardtops presented several structural and engineering challenges. With no support from the roof, the shorter "B" post (seen here) had to be beefed up at the bottom to provide sufficient support for the doors.

To provide room inside the door for the eccentric maneuvering of the window, the rear door had to extend back farther than usual, shown here.

Headlights on the 1955 models were slightly recessed and all models got the Ninety-eight's scooped out front wheel openings. Even the rear fender skirts were partially cut away. This is a Super 88 two-door hardtop, called a Holiday coupe.

1955 was a big year in the industry for brightly contrasting two-tone paint schemes. The designers had to come up with side trim that permitted two toning the body below the belt line, as demonstrated by this Super 88 sedan. Power was boosted to 185 bhp in the 88s, and 202 bhp in the Super 88s and Ninety-eights.

This is the front compartment of a 1955 Ninety-eight sedan. The distortion caused by the acute curvature of the panoramic windshield can be seen through the right side.

This 88 two-door sedan was the lowest priced 1955 Oldsmobile. The "88" emblem near the headlight was one of the few differences between the 88 and the Super 88.

The greater size of the Ninety-eights, in both wheelbase (126 inches vs. 122) and overall length (212 inches vs. 203) is evident in these views of Ninety-eight (bottom) and Super 88 convertibles.

A Ninety-eight Holiday coupe, showing off its flared wheel openings and a no doubt flashy two-tone paint scheme. This was Oldsmobile's finest two-door hardtop. The available air conditioning was moved from the trunk to the dashboard this year.

This is a 1955 Ninety-eight sedan, the most luxurious sedan in the Olds line. This was the only 98 model that continued to use fender skirts. Sales of the new four-door hardtops cut heavily into sales of sedans like these.

In 1956, the bumper grew to completely surround the Olds grill, giving it a slightly fish mouthed look. Yet the heritage was unmistakable and the overall effect was attractive.

For the first time the Super 88 four-door sedan was not the best selling Oldsmobile. The glamorous new Holiday hardtop four-door edged past this sedan model in sales. Horsepower was up again to 240 bhp in the Super 88s and Ninety-eights and 230 bhp in the standard 88. The difference was in carburetion.

Replacing three of the gauges with warning lights permitted the instrument panel to be restyled by making the speedometer and clock faces oval shaped. The central location for the glove compartment was convenient.

This is a 1956 88 two-door sedan, the lowest priced Olds. It was powered by the same legendary Rocket V8 with only fractionally less power than the Super 88. This standard 88 could barely be distinguished from the more expensive and powerful Super 88. The rear fender sash molding was slimmer on the 88 and the numerals on the front fender differed slightly.

Glamorous Holiday hardtops were available in the 88 Series as well. Since the 88s looked and performed like the Super 88s, it is no wonder the cheaper series outsold the Super 88 line for the first time.

Here is a 1956 88 Holiday hardtop sedan. With white sidewall tires and De Luxe wheelcovers, it looks every bit as snazzy as a Super 88. The Super 88 models did have more luxurious interiors with carpeting and finer fabrics.

This is the Ninety-eight version of the Holiday sedan, pictured here in front of the brand new GM Tech Center at Warren, Michigan, near Detroit. Note that the Ninety-eight side trim differs from the 88s.

The sedan version of the Ninety-eight. Wheelbase was still 126 inches, while all 88s rode on a 122-inch wheelbase. Hydra-Matic was modified for 1956 by the addition of a second turbine (fluid coupling). This was claimed to make the transmission smoother. Naturally, that required a new name. It was now called Jetaway Hydra-Matic. Jet and rocket propulsion were popular as advertising themes in the fifties, especially at Oldsmobile.

Here is a two-door Ninety-eight Holiday hardtop, also posed in front of the newly opened GM Tech Center, which was designed by the internationally known architect Eero Saarinen. Those extra cost three-spoke hubcaps came to be highly prized by light-fingered car enthusiasts.

The last word in Oldsmobile glamour for 1956, the Ninety-eight Starfire convertible. This was a year of lower sales for the industry compared to 1955, and Olds built 485,458 cars, down about 100,000 units. This was still good enough for 7.7 percent of the U.S. market, a very respectable showing.

The 1957 Oldsmobiles used the entirely new General Motors "B" body which was shared with Buick Special and Century. GM Styling continued using many of the styling cues Olds had been developing for years, but some were now exaggerated to the point of caricature such as the fish mouth grill and the low belt line. This is a Super 88 four-door sedan.

This 1957 Super 88 Holiday hardtop sedan shows the enlarged "Span-A-Ramic" windshield that extended farther up into the roof and around the corners, to the point where it became more difficult for passengers to get in and out of the front seat without knocking knees on the windshield post.

Unlike previous years, all 1957 Oldsmobile post sedans and hardtops shared the same bodies, sheet metal and roof panels. All models, whether convertible, hardtop, sedan or wagon, used the same doors (four-door models use shorter front doors than two-door models). The purpose was to reduce tooling and production costs, but the result in some models was tight access and reduced side glass area. This was the lowest priced Olds, a "Golden Rocket" two-door sedan. The "Golden" series name had no particular meaning and was used only one year.

This is a 1957 Super 88 Holiday Coupe. The lower belt line forced the side roof line to be dropped, reducing vision for taller people. Wheel size was reduced to 14 inches, another tactic to reduce height.

A 1957 Super 88 convertible posed next to an Oldsmobile curved dash runabout. The runabout was Olds first sales success and was produced from 1901 to about 1906. For 1957, Rocket engine displacement was increased again, this time to 371 cid. Power reached a new high of 277 horsepower and was the same in all models. For a mere $83 extra, a buyer could order the J-2 engine option which used three two barrel carburetors and a 10 to 1 compression ratio to develop 300 bhp.

All sedan and hardtops used this novel three section split rear window. Rear visibility was somewhat impaired by the struts. Prospective buyers didn't like it, so it was quickly dropped the next year. This 88 Holiday coupe demonstrates the increase in the chrome load. The fuel cap was concealed behind the chrome panel under the left taillight.

The new instrument panel had a few bizarre touches. In addition to the blinding chrome, the dash top sloped down toward the windshield and created a trap for small objects left on the dashboard.

The station wagon body style returned to the Oldsmobile line for the first time since 1950. It was available in both 88 Series with either hardtop or post style doors. Wagons were called "Fiestas," a name last used in 1953 for a luxury convertible. This is a Super 88 Fiesta.

The new Olds wagon used a two-piece tailgate, with a truly panoramic rear window in the liftgate.

The 1957 98s continued the formula started in 1952—a four-inch longer wheelbase and a longer rear deck than the 88s. This is a 98 Holiday coupe. The new Olds styling was not popular, and Chrysler Corporation was taking sales with its striking new tailfinned cars. Olds production fell about 100,000 units, to 384,390 cars.

The rear compartment of a 98 Starfire Holiday four-door hardtop shows the high quality trim and upholstery. Note the folding center armrest and electric window lifts. Note also the large center door post and the struts in the rear window.

This is a 1957 98 Holiday Sedan. All 98 models were now called "Starfires," not just the convertible.

This profile view of a 1957 98 convertible shows the extreme to which rear deck length had gone. The great length, coupled with the smaller wheels and cut down doors, combined to give an impression that the middle of the car was dragging.

Poor sales in 1957 inspired GM Stylists to do a hurried make over of the Olds exterior for 1958. Most sheet metal was changed, and a mish-mash of brightwork was slapped on everywhere. Most Oldsmobile design cues, which had served to identify Olds cars for a decade, were hastily abandoned, as demonstrated by the new grill on this Dynamic 88. Quad headlights were new for 1958.

The 1958 Olds restyling was seen by many as a garish, tasteless mess. Few American production cars, before or since, have carried as much chrome. This is a Dynamic 88 Holiday coupe, which actually had less brightwork than the more expensive models. “Dynamic 88” was the new name for the lowest priced Oldsmobiles.

The post sedans again used the same body and doors as the hardtops, as shown by this Dynamic 88 sedan. The elaborate facelift and all that chrome didn't work. Olds sales dropped another 90,000 cars to 296,374.

Put on your sunglasses for a chrome close-up. Some thought the chrome strips on the rear fender of this 98 Holiday coupe resembled a musical score. All that was missing were the notes. The fuel cap was hidden under the fin and chrome ahead of the left taillight.

A Super 88 Holiday hardtop sedan photographed outside the new GM Tech Center. The struts dividing the rear window were removed for 58. Compared to the Dynamic 88, the Super 88s and 98s added extra panels of chrome to the front fenders and even to the roof. The excessive decoration was attributed to Harley Earl, the head of GM Styling who was about to retire. Earl had always favored longer, lower and flashier as design objectives.

A Super 88 Fiesta hardtop wagon posed appropriately in front of a new suburban rambler. Rocket engine horsepower was boosted to 305 bhp in the Super 88 and 98, but reduced to 265 bhp in the Dynamic 88. The J-2 tri-carb manifold was available on any model, and boosted power to 312 bhp.

The 98 Series continued to use a 126-inch wheelbase, four inches longer than the 88s. However, the deck was eight inches longer, especially noticeable on this Holiday coupe. The advertising folks at Olds coined the word "Oldsmobility" to promote the 1958 cars. The definition of the word remains uncertain.

This is a 1958 98 Holiday sedan. Olds, along with other GM Divisions, offered air suspension as an option for 1958. Called "New-Matic" by Olds, few buyers chose it, which was fortunate. The system was complex, troublesome, and offered little advantage over conventional springs. Most air suspension installations were eventually removed and the cars retrofitted with springs.

This happy 1958 Olds 98 convertible driver looks ready for a sunny cruise. The light paint color muted the dazzle of all that chrome a bit. The Starfire name disappeared completely this year, even from the 98 convertible.

After the disastrous designs of many General Motors cars in 1958, Bill Mitchell, the new head of GM Styling, led a complete redesign of all GM cars for 1959. The appearance of the new Oldsmobiles shown here was cleaner and more unified than the 1957 and 1958 cars. The Super 88 Sport Sedan in the back of this photo had a striking new rear window design.

Greatly increased glass area in all body styles was a design theme for the 1959 models. This Super 88 Holiday "SceniCoupe" shows how the rear window extended over the heads of the rear seat occupants. The glass was heavily tinted to reduce heat transfer, but buyers were well advised to order air conditioning on this model.

A Super 88 convertible in a favorite advertising pose at poolside. No explanation was offered as to why an automobile would be allowed on the pool deck. Rocket engine size was increased again for the fourth time since the engine was introduced in 1949. Super 88s and 98s were now 394 cid, while the Dynamic 88 engine remained 371 cid. Horsepower rose to 315 in the Super 88s and 98s.

The most dramatic new body style for 1959 was the Sport Sedan four-door hardtop. Seen here as a Super 88, this body was available in all three Oldsmobile Series. The lowness and great width of the cars is evident here. Wheelbase of 88s grew an inch to 123 inches while 98s remained at 126 inches. Overall length grew to a garage popping 223 inches on the 98s and 218.4 inches on the 88s.

The rear compartment of a Super 88 Sport Sedan four-door hardtop. There was little structure supporting the roof except glass. Overall height of this model was only 54.2 inches, several inches lower than hardtops of just a few years prior. For the first time, rear floors were recessed to provide foot-room for rear seat passengers.

Front seat passengers did not fare so well for foot-room. The roof and seats were just as low as in back, but the floor was not recessed. The gigantic new windshield curved up into the roof and still retained a knee knocking windshield post. This is a 98 four-door.

The station wagon was completely redesigned and enlarged. Cargo space grew by 13 percent and cargo length by 8 inches. Hardtop style windows were dropped. The wagon was available in both 88 Series.

At the rear, the separate liftgate was eliminated and replaced with a rear window that rolled down into the tailgate. There was plenty of cargo deck space here, but the low roof limited the height of objects that could be carried.

The 1959 window post sedan bodies reverted to using a roof panel that was different from hardtop models. The result was a higher roofline on the sedans and a more spacious feeling interior. This is a 98 four-door sedan.

As in most years, the 1959 98 convertible was the glamour leader of the Oldsmobile line. Upholstery was still top quality hand buffed leather at a time when many competitors had switched to vinyl. Use of an anamorphic camera lens made the car look even longer and lower.

With all of its glass area, the 1959 Olds 98 Holiday "SceniCoupe" felt almost as open as a top down convertible. The new styling brought a rebound in sales. Production was up 86,490 cars to a total of 382,864 Oldsmobiles.

For 1960, Oldsmobiles got revised exterior sheet metal and trim, but were little changed mechanically. This view of a Super 88 sedan shows how the windshield extended into the roof. Horsepower and engine displacement of the Super 88 and 98 remained the same at 315 bhp and 394 cid.

This is a 1960 Super 88 Holiday SceniCoupe. The cleaner, more restrained side trim was a refreshing contrast to the Oldsmobiles of 1957 and 1958. Overall length was actually reduced by almost one inch! This signaled the start of a return in the sixties to more moderately sized cars.

The vast rear window of this 1960 Super 88 two-door hardtop illustrates where the name "SceniCoupe" came from. The rear deck looks large enough to be a helicopter launch pad. The flared rear bumper was a distinctive change.

Super 88 convertibles like the one shown, as well as the 98 convertibles, continued to use quality leather upholstery. Wheelbase of 88s and 98s remained unchanged at 123 inches and 126 inches respectively.

The enlarged new station wagon introduced in 1959 was continued in 1960. This is a Dynamic 88. The standard equipment engine in the Dynamic Series was a lower power 240 bhp 371 cid Rocket V8 claimed to be more economical.

A new wagon option for 1960 was a rear facing third seat. This was an innovation first offered by Chrysler Corporation in 1957. Entry was over the tailgate; note the steps by the back up lights. Door gates to make rear entry easier would not appear until the mid-sixties.

The 1960 98s were difficult to distinguish from the 88s, but were three inches longer in length and wheelbase. This is a Holiday Sportsedan.

The rear view of Oldsmobile's top line four-door hardtop, the 98 Holiday Sportsedan. The unique overhanging rear roof line harmonized well with the equally unique flared rear bumper

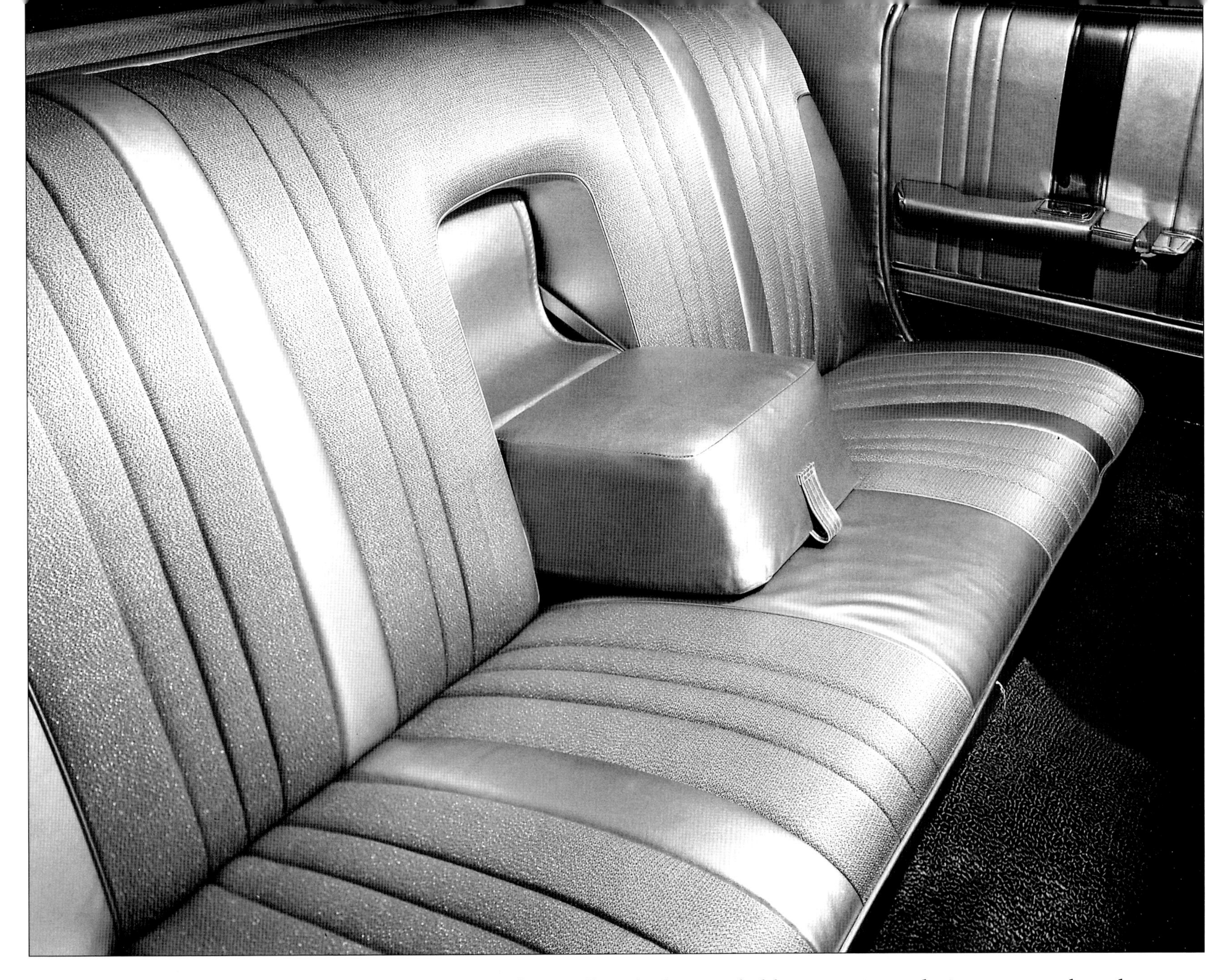

The plush rear seat of a 98 Sportsedan. Note the foot wells, which provided leg room in a what was a very low slung car. Olds production for 1960 totaled 347,365 cars, down some from 1959. Car buyers were turning away from large medium priced cars to smaller, economical imports and compact cars.

This happy young woman heading down the road in a handsome 1960 98 convertible symbolizes the journey ahead for Olds, down the roads of the sixties and seventies. It would be a time of unprecedented growth and success for Oldsmobile Division.

AUTOMOTIVE

AMC Cars 1954-1987: An Illustrated History ..... ISBN 1-58388-112-3
AMC Performance Cars 1951-1983 Photo Archive ..... ISBN 1-58388-127-1
AMX Photo Archive: From Concept to Reality ..... ISBN 1-58388-062-3
Camaro 1967-2000 Photo Archive ..... ISBN 1-58388-032-1
Checker Cab Co. Photo History ..... ISBN 1-58388-100-X
Chevrolet Corvair Photo History ..... ISBN 1-58388-118-2
Chevrolet Station Wagons 1946-1966 Photo Archive ..... ISBN 1-58388-069-0
Classic American Limousines 1955-2000 Photo Archive ..... ISBN 1-58388-041-0
The Complete U.S. Automotive Sales Literature Checklist 1946-2000 ..... ISBN 1-58388-155-7
Cord Automobiles L-29 & 810/812 Photo Archive ..... ISBN 1-58388-102-6
Corvair by Chevrolet Experimental & Production Cars 1957-1969, Ludvigsen Library Series ..... ISBN 1-58388-058-5
Corvette The Exotic Experimental Cars, Ludvigsen Library Series ..... ISBN 1-58388-017-8
Corvette Prototypes & Show Cars Photo Album ..... ISBN 1-882256-77-8
Duesenberg Racecars and Passenger Cars Photo Archive ..... ISBN 1-58388-145-X
Early Ford V-8s 1932-1942 Photo Album ..... ISBN 1-882256-97-2
Ferrari- The Factory Maranello's Secrets 1950-1975, Ludvigsen Library Series ..... ISBN 1-58388-085-2
Ford Postwar Flatheads 1946-1953 Photo Archive ..... ISBN 1-58388-080-1
Ford Station Wagons 1929-1991 Photo History ..... ISBN 1-58388-103-4
Hudson Automobiles 1934-1957 Photo Archive ..... ISBN 1-58388-110-7
Imperial 1955-1963 Photo Archive ..... ISBN 1-882256-22-0
Imperial 1964-1968 Photo Archive ..... ISBN 1-882256-23-9
Jaguar XK120, XK140, XK150 Sports Cars Ludvigsen Library Series ..... ISBN 1-58388-150-6
Javelin Photo Archive: From Concept to Reality ..... ISBN 1-58388-071-2
The Lincoln Continental Story: From Zephyr to Mark II ..... ISBN 1-58388-154-9
Lincoln Motor Cars 1920-1942 Photo Archive ..... ISBN 1-882256-57-3
Lincoln Motor Cars 1946-1960 Photo Archive ..... ISBN 1-882256-58-1
Mercedes-Benz 300SL: Gullings and Roadsters 1954-1964 Ludvigsen Library Series ..... ISBN 1-58388-137-9
MG Saloons and Coupes 1925-1980 ..... ISBN 1-58388-144-1
Nash 1936-1957 Photo Archive ..... ISBN 1-58388-086-0
Oldsmobile 1946-1960 Photo Archive ..... ISBN 1-58388-168-9
Packard Motor Cars 1946-1958 Photo Archive ..... ISBN 1-882256-45-X
Pontiac Dream Cars, Show Cars & Prototypes 1928-1998 Photo Album ..... ISBN 1-882256-93-X
Pontiac Firebird Trans-Am 1969-1999 Photo Album ..... ISBN 1-882256-95-6
Pontiac Firebird 1967-2000 Photo History ..... ISBN 1-58388-028-3
Pontiac's Greatest Decade 1959-1969—The Wide Track Era: An Illustrated History ..... ISBN 1-58388-163-8
Rambler 1950-1969 Photo Archive ..... ISBN 1-58388-078-X
Stretch Limousines 1928-2001 Photo Archive ..... ISBN 1-58388-070-4
Studebaker 1933-1942 Photo Archive ..... ISBN 1-882256-24-7
Studebaker Hawk 1956-1964 Photo Archive ..... ISBN 1-58388-094-1
Studebaker Lark 1959-1966 Photo Archive ..... ISBN 1-58388-107-7
Thirty Years of the Volkswagen Golf & Rabbit ..... ISBN 1-58388-158-1
Ultimate Corvette Trivia Challenge ..... ISBN 1-58388-035-6

RACING

Can-Am Racing Cars: Secrets of the Sensational Sixties Sports-Racers ..... ISBN 1-58388-134-4
Chaparral Can-Am Racing Cars from Texas, Ludvigsen Library Series ..... ISBN 1-58388-066-6
Cunningham Sports Cars, Ludvigsen Library Series ..... ISBN 1-58388-109-3
Drag Racing Funny Cars of the 1970s Photo Archive ..... ISBN 1-58388-068-2
Indy Cars 1911-1939: Great Racers from the Crucible of Speed Ludvigsen Library Series ..... ISBN 1-58388-151-4
Indy Cars of the 1940s, Ludvigsen Library Series ..... ISBN 1-58388-117-4
Indy Cars of the 1950s, Ludvigsen Library Series ..... ISBN 1-58388-018-6
Indy Cars of the 1960s, Ludvigsen Library Series ..... ISBN 1-58388-052-6
Indy Cars of the 1970s, Ludvigsen Library Series ..... ISBN 1-58388-098-4
Indianapolis Racing Cars of Frank Kurtis 1941-1963 Photo Archive ..... ISBN 1-58388-026-7
Lost Race Tracks Treasures of Automobile Racing ..... ISBN 1-58388-084-4
Marvelous Mechanical Designs of Harry A. Miller ..... ISBN 1-58388-123-9
Mercedes-Benz 300SL Racing Cars 1952-1953, Ludvigsen Library Series ..... ISBN 1-58388-067-4
Mercedes-Benz 300SLR: The Fabulous 1955 World-Champion Sports-Racer ..... ISBN 1-58388-122-0
MG Competition Cars and Drivers ..... ISBN 1-58388-166-2
MG Record-Breakers from Abingdon Photo Archive ..... ISBN 1-58388-116-6
Novi V-8 Indy Cars 1941-1965, Ludvigsen Library Series ..... ISBN 1-58388-037-2
Porsche Spyders Type 550 1953-1956, Ludvigsen Library Series ..... ISBN 1-58388-092-5
Pro-Stock Drag Racing of the 1970s: From Stockers to Doorslammers ..... ISBN 1-58388-141-7
Sebring 12-Hour Race 1970 Photo Archive ..... ISBN 1-882256-20-4
Slingshot Dragsters of the 1960s Photo Archive ..... ISBN 1-58388-148-4
Top Fuel Dragsters of the 1970s Photo Archive ..... ISBN 1-58388-128-X
Vanderbilt Cup Race 1936 & 1937 Photo Archive ..... ISBN 1-882256-66-2

More Great Titles From Iconografix

All Iconografix books are available from direct mail specialty book dealers and bookstores worldwide, or can be ordered from the publisher. For book trade and distribution information or to add your name to our mailing list and receive a **FREE CATALOG** contact:

Iconografix, Inc.
PO Box 446, Dept BK
Hudson, WI, 54016

Telephone: (715) 381-9755,
(800) 289-3504 (USA),
Fax: (715) 381-9756
info@iconografixinc.com
www.iconografixinc.com

TRUCKS

AM General: Hummers, Mutts, Buses & Postal Jeeps ..... ISBN 1-58388-135-2
Autocar Trucks 1899-1950 Photo Archive ..... ISBN 1-58388-115-8
Autocar Trucks 1950-1987 Photo Archive ..... ISBN 1-58388-072-0
Beverage Trucks 1910-1975 Photo Archive ..... ISBN 1-882256-60-3
*Brockway Trucks 1948-1961 Photo Archive** ..... ISBN 1-882256-55-7
Chevrolet El Camino Photo History Incl. GMC Sprint & Caballero ..... ISBN 1-58388-044-5
Circus and Carnival Trucks 1923-2000 Photo Archive ..... ISBN 1-58388-048-8
Dodge B-Series Trucks Restorer's & Collector's Reference Guide and History ..... ISBN 1-58388-087-9
Dodge C-Series Trucks Restorer's & Collector's Reference Guide and History ..... ISBN 1-58388-140-9
Dodge Pickups 1939-1978 Photo Album ..... ISBN 1-882256-82-4
Dodge Power Wagons 1940-1980 Photo Archive ..... ISBN 1-882256-89-1
Dodge Power Wagon Photo History ..... ISBN 1-58388-019-4
Dodge Ram Trucks 1994-2001 Photo History ..... ISBN 1-58388-051-8
Dodge Trucks 1929-1947 Photo Archive ..... ISBN 1-882256-36-0
Dodge Trucks 1948-1960 Photo Archive ..... ISBN 1-882256-37-9
Ford 4x4s 1935-1990 Photo History ..... ISBN 1-58388-079-8
Ford Heavy-Duty Trucks 1948-1998 Photo History ..... ISBN 1-58388-043-7
Ford Medium-Duty Trucks 1917-1998 Photo History ..... ISBN 1-58388-162-X
Ford Ranchero 1957-1979 Photo History ..... ISBN 1-58388-126-3
Freightliner Trucks 1937-1981 Photo Archive ..... ISBN 1-58388-090-9
FWD Trucks 1910-1974 Photo Archive ..... ISBN 1-58388-142-5
GMC Heavy-Duty Trucks 1927-1987 ..... ISBN 1-58388-125-5
International Heavy Trucks of the 1950s: At Work ..... ISBN 1-58388-160-3
International Heavy Trucks of the 1960s: At Work ..... ISBN 1-58388-161-1
Jeep 1941-2000 Photo Archive ..... ISBN 1-58388-021-6
Jeep Prototypes & Concept Vehicles Photo Archive ..... ISBN 1-58388-033-X
Kenworth Trucks 1950-1979 At Work ..... ISBN 1-58388-147-6
*Mack Model AB Photo Archive** ..... ISBN 1-882256-18-2
*Mack AP Super-Duty Trucks 1926-1938 Photo Archive** ..... ISBN 1-882256-54-9
*Mack Model B 1953-1966 Volume 2 Photo Archive** ..... ISBN 1-882256-34-4
*Mack EB-EC-ED-EE-EF-EG-DE 1936-1951 Photo Archive** ..... ISBN 1-882256-29-8
*Mack FC-FCSW-NW 1936-1947 Photo Archive** ..... ISBN 1-882256-28-X
*Mack FG-FH-FJ-FK-FN-FP-FT-FW 1937-1950 Photo Archive** ..... ISBN 1-882256-35-2
*Mack LF-LH-LJ-LM-LT 1940-1956 Photo Archive** ..... ISBN 1-882256-38-7
*Mack Trucks Photo Gallery** ..... ISBN 1-882256-88-3
New Car Carriers 1910-1998 Photo Album ..... ISBN 1-882256-98-0
Peterbilt Trucks 1939-1979 At Work ..... ISBN 1-58388-152-2
Refuse Trucks Photo Archive ..... ISBN 1-58388-042-9
Studebaker Trucks 1927-1940 Photo Archive ..... ISBN 1-882256-40-9
White Trucks 1900-1937 Photo Archive ..... ISBN 1-882256-80-8

BUSES

Buses of ACF Photo Archive Including ACF-Brill And CCF-Brill ..... ISBN 1-58388-101-8
Buses of Motor Coach Industries 1932-2000 Photo Archive ..... ISBN 1-58388-039-9
City Transit Buses of the 20th Century Photo Gallery ..... ISBN 1-58388-146-8
Fageol & Twin Coach Buses 1922-1956 Photo Archive ..... ISBN 1-58388-075-5
Flxible Intercity Buses 1924-1970 Photo Archive ..... ISBN 1-58388-108-5
Flxible Transit Buses 1953-1995 Photo Archive ..... ISBN 1-58388-053-4
GM Intercity Coaches 1944-1980 Photo Archive ..... ISBN 1-58388-099-2
Greyhound in Postcards: Buses, Depots and Posthouses ..... ISBN 1-58388-130-1
Highway Buses of the 20th Century Photo Gallery ..... ISBN 1-58388-121-2
*Mack® Buses 1900-1960 Photo Archive** ..... ISBN 1-58388-020-8
New York City Transit Buses 1945-1975 Photo Archive ..... ISBN 1-58388-149-2
Prevost Buses 1924-2002 Photo Archive ..... ISBN 1-58388-083-6
Trailways Buses 1936-2001 Photo Archive ..... ISBN 1-58388-029-1
Trolley Buses 1913-2001 Photo Archive ..... ISBN 1-58388-057-7
Welcome Aboard the GM New Look Bus: An Enthusiast's Reference ..... ISBN 1-58388-167-0
Yellow Coach Buses 1923-1943 Photo Archive ..... ISBN 1-58388-054-2

RECREATIONAL VEHICLES & OTHER

Commercial Ships on the Great Lakes Photo Gallery ..... ISBN 1-58388-153-0
Phillips 66 1945-1954 Photo Archive ..... ISBN 1-882256-42-5
RVs & Campers 1900-2000: An Illustrated History ..... ISBN 1-58388-064-X
Ski-Doo Racing Sleds 1960-2003 Photo Archive ..... ISBN 1-58388-105-0
The Collector's Guide to Ski-Doo Snowmobiles ..... ISBN 1-58388-133-6